I0756014

FINISHING LINE PRESS
www.finishinglinepress.com

The Race for Daphne

poems by

Sarah C. Beckmann

Finishing Line Press
Georgetown, Kentucky

The Race for Daphne

ISBN 979-8-89990-458-5 First Edition

ACKNOWLEDGMENTS

"DOE *v.* DISTRICT: APPLE FOR THE DISTRICT" has been selected by the City of Boston (in conjunction with the Mayor's Office of Arts & Culture) to appear in *In the Life and Time of*, an anthology curated by former Boston Poet Laureate Porsha Olayiwola.

"Frances Ann" has been accepted to appear in *We've Always Done It!: Poems About Wartime Women*, an anthology produced by Alternating Current Press.

I'd like to recognize the following family members who contributed to the creation of this collection, whether I interviewed them as part of my genealogy research, or for simply supporting me throughout the years: both of my parents, Susan and Rich Beckmann; my aunt Penny Steindl; my cousin Vicki Waxenberg; my uncle Kim Harwood; my cousin Susie Serreze; my cousin Anna Pelosi; in memory of my grandfather Dick Beckmann and aunt Jean Davidson—and so many more people who have loved and nurtured me.

I want to acknowledge the poetic ancestors and modern writers whose traditions I've inherited, and whose work I've been moved by, while producing this book: Anne Bradstreet, Emma Lazarus, Walt Whitman, W.B. Yeats, Gwendolyn Brooks, Robert Hayden, Eavan Boland, Natasha Trethewey, and Paul Tran.

Credit is also due to my graduate professors Dan Tobin and Christine Casson, who have been invaluable mentors to me, in the classroom and out of it. To my community of fellow Boston writers, including Livia Meneghin, Tatiana Johnson-Boria, and Porsha Olayiwola, among others: thank you for constantly pushing me and inspiring me with your work. Lastly, to my coworkers at MIT, my personal friends, and my partner Morgan—thank you. You teach me much, too.

Publisher: Leah Huete de Maines
Editor: Christen Kincaid
Cover Art: Julia Paccone
Author Photo: Bhumika Choudhary
Cover Design: Elizabeth Maines McCleavy

Order online: www.finishinglinepress.com
also available on amazon.com

Author inquiries and mail orders:
Finishing Line Press
PO Box 1626
Georgetown, Kentucky 40324
USA

Contents

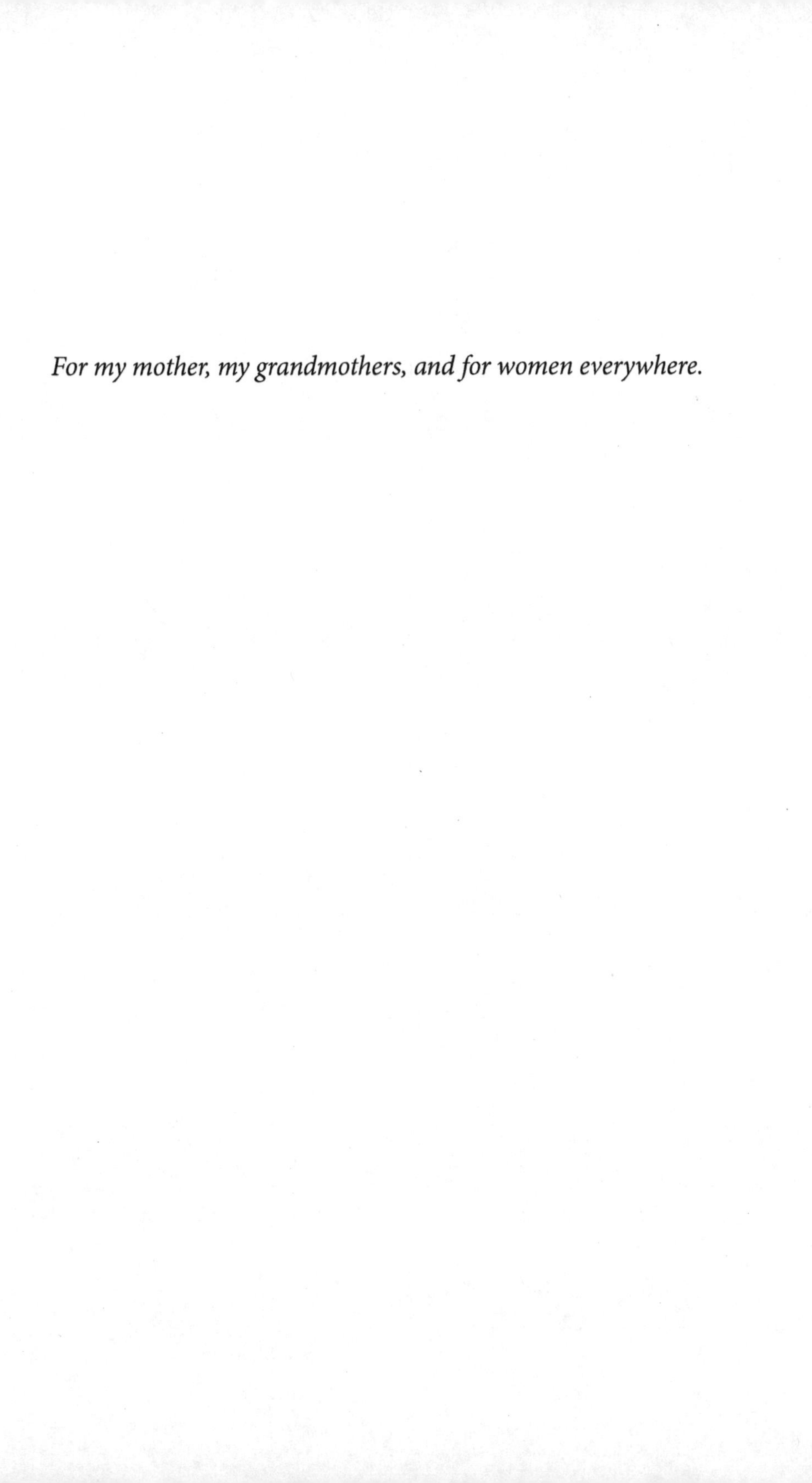

For my mother, my grandmothers, and for women everywhere.

Medusa with the Head of Perseus

by Luciano Garbati (2008); on display October 13, 2020–April 30, 2021

Perseus may have my head in his hand,
raised like a prize, somewhere in Florence,
but I don't recall what I did to anger him.
I never liked the gods, nor their spawn.

If you cross the Atlantic, pass Ellis Island,
to the heart of New York: Collect Pond Park,
across from a courthouse, on a pedestal,
wearing droplets of dew like diamonds—

that's the real me—

my gaze wreaks stone, and to stone I stand.
One fist grips his hair; the other, his sword.
My stance, wide, snakes swept to one side,
shoulders back and chin down, daring you
to *look*.

When they say my name
you hear *monster*—you can't tear
your eyes away—can you?—look on,
and know my version of the tale. Give me

your weary, your broken, your abandoned
and idol-less; Hercules and Theseus can come
at their own risk. I'm a sister to exiles, mother
of the She. All I ask is

who are the heroes now

First 500 meters: Midsummer

"In a way, a [2,000-meter Olympic standard] crew race was a play divided up into four acts—the start, the settle, the middle, and the sprint."

—Daniel J. Boyne

Starting from Southold

Starting from fish-shape Paumanok, where I was born...
—Walt Whitman

I.

I entered quietly into this world,
hazel eyes wide and both fists
full of snakes that slid into my crib
the moment they got wind
that I might become a woman.

As they died, they hissed in my new
ears, bidding me listen to their lies.
Even then I knew not to trust them.

I've lived in Eden all my life, but
those rattling voices stay with me,
follow wherever I go. Should I
make a wig from their carcasses?
Become the monster they told me
I could never avoid becoming.

Later I learned that women have
always worn this writhing wreath;
our knowledge is deep-seeded, and I
intend to plant different beginnings
in this garden—relying less on fate
and fable. More on hard little rocks
of choice, on ever-flowering trial.

II.

At the bottom edge of the hamlet,
at the end of South Harbor Road,
a sacred site: horse flies, humid low tide,

a narrow footpath that leads to sand
bright as snow in the sun, red umbrellas
camped straight ahead. Among goose dung
and seaweed, I string shells on reeds,
wear them like jewels; a metallic necklace
on my collarbone, gems adorning my wrists
and ankles. I walk not just in my own steps—

generations of family and friends march
with me to this place that holds us
like a mother, births us into burned bathers
every summer. Caught in the talons
of an osprey, I will never stop coming here,
will baptize myself in this balmy bay year
after year, in the channel between us and the tip
of Indian Neck, that gleaming strip of paradise.

Some squirm at spider crabs, but all I know
is these waters are primordial; the simple
idea of me washed up on this shoreline
like a dark-haired Venus, shrouded in foam,
pearly nacre eyes closed and dreaming

of fields and vines. Of being dug up from
the roots and harvested like a ripe tomato,
of being husked from wispy head to stalk,
naked kernels glimmering yellow. My heart
was a greenhouse, made of glass and growing
warm, wild things. Letting only light in,

not knowing of darkness.

My Mother Grew Up in Babylon

in a small house designed by her father. A civil
engineer with the eye of an architect, he cut a garage
into a hill beneath the first floor, and built six rooms—
simple, and whole, which is what both her parents

needed. They polished the wood of the living room's
back wall with oil—my mother can still smell it—
waxed the kitchen cabinets with Jubilee, used Preen
on the floors, as if products could wipe away grief

and keep the past at bay. But some things her parents
could never discard. The unfinished second story
soon became storage for their sorrows: in one corner,
a shrine to her father's first wife, who died in childbirth

(piles of jewelry, platinum rings for petite fingers);
in another, memorabilia from his second wife who died
of cancer (he'd kept her nursing uniforms starched
and white); in another, my grandmother's first wedding

dress hung in a cream satin tent, but traveled nowhere
in that palanquin—the knowledge that her ex-husband
still walked the earth after leaving her was somehow
worse than death. My mother has dreams of that attic,

of finding hidden treasures there, even though it's been
years since her parents died, the house cleared. Maybe
the lofts of all our minds look something like this.
Maybe my grandmother took solace in their yard,

in the garden filled with azaleas, in the honeysuckle
my mother used to sip. Babylon, for her, was a haven.
I'm certain, almost, that when my grandmother looked
at the dogwood tree in their yard, at the twisted bark,

at the red mark that stained each of the four white
petals of its flower, blooming early every spring—
when she held my mother's face in her hands—
she thought not just of sacrifice

but of a second chance.

Joan of Merrick

From an early age you learned that war
comes in many forms. As first-born

daughter and natural leader, you spoke
loudly often; your mother told you to be

quieter, but demureness was never part
of your character. You thrived in choir,

and when you weren't in school, you
were upstate at Camp of the Woods;

Lake Pleasant, a beautiful backdrop
to the *worth-while* skills you learned:

sewing lessons led to making dresses,
fed obsession with fabric, string, buttons,

machines, zippers—you fought to the top
of a local department store with needle

in hand. Battle maps, military strategy
covered the dining table as you competed

for scholarship at Tobé–Coburn School
for Fashion Careers; they knew a general

when they saw one, and you commanded
Abraham & Straus, Bloomingdales,

to the store you started above the A&P
grocery in Rochester called The Merry-

Go-Round, where you sold handmade
children's clothing. Retail legend has it

that, by the time you ended your career
as store manager at Bergdorf Goodman,

people hushed at your name, respected you
with a mix of awe and fear. All the while, you and

your husband took my father and aunt
cross country, camping out the back

of your station wagon; summered
out east on Long Island with life-

long friends; became godparents
to nine more children. You shined

brightest at Christmas, making
mounds of cookies, stollen, trifle,

panettone—main roasts of goose,
turkey, ham, beef, or duck. Piled

plates were works of art, with
colors complimenting each other.

Your bread pudding had a single
almond in it; whoever, you said,

found the almond would have
good luck for the year (you added

more than one almond and made
sure they were found by the people

who needed them most). You poured
brandy over plum pudding and lit

the whole thing on fire—a toast
with sparkling burgundy in crystal

glasses!—but you could always
stop to smell—

the bearded iris your mother raised
in the garden at Merrick. I imagine you

sitting beneath the weeping willow
in the front yard, strawberry blond hair
dipping to your knees, hugged against
your chest, cream skin peeking from
a homemade dress—and find myself
weeping, too. You wove such vibrant
threads through life's tapestry; I trace
them with my hands, still the child
you knew, wishing you could see
the woman I've become. Grandmother,

I kneel before you in the grass, armored
in the chainmail you knit me. Knight me
as my name demands—not as princess, but
inheritor of something greater than I can
understand. Tell me: if I commit to this
cause, if I don that helm one day, how

does the beloved learn to love?
What becomes of a matriarch?

Frances Ann

For my aunt

For this poem I call on Melpomene, muse of tragedy.
From birth, your life has been more like a cancer,
a mass in your chest that keeps multiplying tragedies.
You're the unwanted, unlucky daughter, but the tragedy
began before your time. Your mother, abandoned
at an early age when her mother died, felt tragedy
follow her like the shadow of Saint Anthony, tragic
patron of the lost. She never journeyed to Heidelberg,
but she always flinched at that name—*Heidelberg*—
the word pierced her like a bullet, a catastrophic
reminder of your father. The world warred and men
like him got drafted, men like him fancied German

women. On his army papers, the ones that men
used to send home, he left your mother heartbroken
by listing her as his sister, not his wife. To that man,
in print, you were not his. You carried the man's
name all your life like a red-hot brand, like a tumor.
Did he feel remorse, as he crouched with gunmen—
as your mother toiled for divorce at a time when women
didn't do that sort of thing? Suddenly marooned
on an island with you, she might've resented loneliness
but didn't let you drown. She found a kinder man,
had my mother. By then you dreamed of Heidelberg,
of taking classes at the university in Heidelberg,

of scaling the sandstone ruins of Heidelberg
castle—that staunch, romantic *schloss* the sandman
could hardly conjure. You spent years in Heidelberg,
strumming guitars in the *Marktplatz*, until Heidelberg
began to feel like home, and all of your tribulation
faded as you walked the *Hauptstrasse* of Heidelberg,
sipping coffee from the quaint cafes in Heidelberg.
But your father's face, to this day, looms malignant
in your mind. He cut you out, like a cancer—
yet your heart still hoped to find him in Heidelberg,
that he'd look into your eyes, promise not to leave.

You were rubble on a hill, and his back was turned.

I can only imagine what carrying that rejection
must have felt like, that sharp piece of Heidelberg
heavy in your pocket. You buried your abandonment
in the military, learned languages, but abandonment
is its own tongue; you were becoming fluent. The man
you married was an army captain—you abandoned
your heart to him, admired how he fought with abandon
in Vietnam. When he returned, you saw the calamity
and clouds of napalm in his eyes. He swallowed tragedy
with drink. Fire burned your house the night he left
you and your son. My mother tried to clear the sickly
smoke from your lungs, but she couldn't kill this virus;

you inherited this story. Your first bout of breast cancer
put flesh to your scars, and we knew medicine alone
could not heal you. My mother gave a name to disease
like yours long ago; she fought against the malady
of brokenness, and shielded me. I visited Heidelberg
and thought of you, but I didn't know the affliction
you suffered, how those memories gather like cells
and haunt you. Piles of paper insulate you—talismans
against the onslaught of daily life, against the men,
the world that wronged you. My mother and I see cancer
for what it is: a mix of necrosis, paranoia, and tragedy.
But who else can you trust with your tragedy

besides us? *We are your chorus!* I sing your trauma,
lift the twisted mask from your face and replace cancer
with a crown of cypress, grateful my mother abandoned
the pattern—grieving that you couldn't. In Heidelberg,
in heaven, know the arms around you are women's.

Second 500 meters: Autumn

The placement of the rowers (the 'rig') of the boat has some simple dynamical consequences for the motion of the boat...The traditional rig for a rowing Eight has a significant non-zero moment and a counter-productive transverse wiggle for the cox to counter...two zero-moment rigs found here, (a) and (d), appear to be new...[this rig] is special because it manages to have a quadruple tandem configuration with a same-side Four positioned inside two same-side pairs.

—John D. Barrow, Centre for Mathematical Sciences,
University of Cambridge

Cox. Sarah

I sing for heroes who have no songs.
I pin them to the page—they are mine,
as I am theirs, in life's endless race.
I am coxswain of this shell; I sit in the stern,
in the present, facing the direction
of motion, facing the future, though as I look
bow-wards, the past stares back at me:
a crew of eight women in a lethal lineup,
their backs to what's coming, and their eyes,
their trust, on me. We all have people who carry us
to this moment, and these are the women
who are always in my boat. My mothers and I—
muses, undines, goddesses sitting in those
nine seats—we are daughters of memory.

8. Susan

Of these daughters of memory, stroke seat
is my maker, a poet in her own right, my strongest
bond in the boat—as much a boat, as a womb,
where we all first learn rhythm: a mother's heart
beating blood and water. She sits facing me,
reflecting my hazel gaze, her light sustaining me
in ways I can't explain. Bathed in olive oil
at birth, her skin radiates intrinsic heat, her voice
rocks me to sleep—the link between us starts
at my navel, and I am forever in her orbit.
She keeps this ship balanced, yet like all heroes,
her flaw is fatal: her love knows no bounds,
but a star can only give so much before
burning out. To know her is to know the sun.

7. Joan

In seven, burning like a goddess of the sun,
my father's mother sits, blue eyes all-knowing
as she takes her strokes. She died years ago
and tended her children like her gardens;
we grew lush in her nurture—her touch still
echoes in our roots. Like birds she used to watch,
our minds migrate back to her, our hearts recall
her song, soft as a swan that wanders into calm
waters. She honed our childhoods into, not gold,
but perfect diamonds. I'll never take for granted
the feeling of her whispering lips, or a plate
steaming with something that always tastes good;
ambrosia for the body, nectar for the soul.
Her love was a gift. In dreams, she winks at me.

6. Assunta

In six seat, in dreams, my mother's mother winks at me
with a black-olive iris. Her hands turn sheets of pasta
through her machine's metal rollers. In her *cucina*,
in her soul, there's only room for blessings—
no space for more heartbreak, no time for tragedy
to lace her consciousness like red coulis on panna cotta.
The few years I knew her, life was *abbondanza*,
sweet as the plump bells of lily-of-the-valley—
but she hung over my mother like that bonnet bud
and almost drowned her in shade. She wore
victimhood like a veil, and taught my mother love
could be conditional, so long as her daughter swore
everything I do is in service to you. In a flood
of affliction, her mother couldn't handle the oar.

5. Alice

In five, my father's father's mother handles the oar
like an ox, square and sure. A painter, geologist,
adventurer, her father a poet and Methodist preacher,
she wasn't known as a cook—burned meat black—
but she loved boating and making people smile.
You'd find her in the Library of Congress collecting
boxes worth of research on the origins of Yankee
Doodle, a proud daughter of the American Revolution,
her husband a Long Island ping pong champion
(but they never bragged). She often thought walls
would say a lot if they could talk, and I wish I had
known her. In my mind: a picture of my grandfather
sitting on the stone of his parents' grave in Franklin,
North Carolina. Legs crossed, eating a sandwich.

4. Ruth

My father's mother's mother sits legs crossed in four seat,
prim and proper. Over ballet or piano lessons, she preferred
basketball, tennis, and riding horses—a student-athlete
from the start. She plucked the Hawaiian guitar, observed
her father and brothers play cricket in Prospect Park,
in Brooklyn. She made homemaking and childrearing
her business, a career she could afford to embark—
but of her children, my grandmother had trouble adhering
to her stubborn laws. *Sit up, speak softer*, her mother said,
spinning in her rigid world of right and wrong—
disapproving of the man her daughter wanted to wed,
unknowing (or knowing) of my father forming along
in the womb—she made my grandmother choose
between the love of her life or the family she knew.

3. Edith

In three, in love with life, my mother's father's mother
smokes a cigarette plugged into a sterling silver filter
with a martini in the other hand. She traveled with her third
and final husband, an engineer on the railroads, as a nurse
who took care of communities that had no physicians
and as a photographer during a time when family portraits,
and cinematography, were new concepts. She bedecked
her tall, strong frame in jewelry, perfumes, and fine clothing;
my mother remembers her hair, a yellow-white curtain
hanging down to her waist, always washed, combed,
and braided, then curled into a bun. A picture of me
on my first birthday (bald, mouth side lopped) sitting before
a Grandma Dede cake: white sponge, buttercream icing
dotted with red cinnamon candy. Her spirit behind the camera.

2. Sarah

A camera—dotted, blurry—might have captured
my mother's mother's mother in two seat, but I've
never seen those pictures. Enigmatic, she sits far
from me in the bow of the boat—just within hearing
of my voice. I shout to her, attempt to span the time
and space between us: a 1920 New York City census
lists her as 36 years old, married to Cono, mother
of eight. She died when my grandmother was young.
Instead of images, I have the mirror, a rectangular
portal to what might have been: is that her in the curve
of my upper lip? In the hair above my nose's bridge
yearning to unify my brows? The faded brown mark
on my forehead, the brush of her thumb? I know little
to nothing of who she was—but I bear her name.

1. Daughter

I know nothing of you, future daughter; your name,
your face, your character are furthest away from me
at this time, but you're on my mind. You are both past
and prologue, a nexus of unknown, and this lineup
is as much your legacy as mine. One day, the cycle
may rotate (I grow quiet and relinquish my role
as coxswain, prepare to heed a new voice as I step
into your shell, take my place in stroke, and watch
as you grip the steering knobs of your own vessel.
Your speech cleaves the silence, save the sound
of oarlocks snapping together). One day, I may row
knowing what I pull through that flat, glassy water
is precious and powerful. I can only hope that you,
too, might sing for women who have no songs.

Third 500 meters: Winter

"Think of sweet and chocolate,
Left to folly or to fate,
Whom the higher gods forgot,
Whom the lower gods berate;
Physical and underfed
Fancying on the featherbed
What was never and is not."

—Gwendolyn Brooks, "The Anniad," *Annie Allen*

STOVE SEQUENCE

I.

In the winter, in the backyard, dad built us an ice rink,
hammered two-by-ten, two-by-twelve, pressure-treated
wooden boards into a frame. Within it he laid one large
sheet of plastic; overnight, he used the hose, filling it
'til it froze. When we invited our friends for a skate,

we could depend on a solid bonfire. He'd start with
twigs, dry pine needles, empty cardboard boxes,
and newspaper, before the logs—they hissed as snow
evaporated from the bark. We huddled on benches,
sipped hot chocolate, our faces flushed and puckered
from smoke that curled through the trees hanging over

our stone-circled pit. I remember smoke puffing
from pipes installed on either side of our house. Not
chimneys, but venting systems for the two beating,
breathing hearts within: our pellet stoves were cheaper,
more pleasant alternatives to the green tank of propane
that sat like a submarine behind the house.

Of all his responsibilities, my dad put this one first:
in the cold, he kept us warm. He kept our fires.

II.

Dad rarely left home. One time, before he did,
he showed me how to keep the stoves. I gained
new appreciation for the process as I hauled
a forty-pound bag of pellets through the garage,

to the basement, and up a flight of stairs. Pellets
come in pallets: fifty bags per pallet—one ton.
We burn four tons a year of nothing but the best:
Northern Warmth Supreme Douglass Fir quarter-

inch pellets made of Oregon softwood, yielding
high heat and low ash—the preferred diet of the
Enviro Empress, a cast iron goddess weighing in
at 480 pounds. Coal black, jaw square, stocky,

and braw, she squats on her heels in the basement
offering heat and ambience. Her hopper holds 60
pounds of sawdust fuel; I open her lid and fill her
to the brim, then hit power on her control pane.

She can be temperamental, dad says. She doesn't
take the bait, so I get on my hands and knees,
whisper a prayer before opening her broad door,
lift the hinge to unbolt her glass eye (avoid her

gaze), clear the caked soot from her burn pot, pay
homage to her inner auger—the motor gyrating
her heart, her convection fan. I don't mention how
her smog stains the paint outside as I present

a gift: a handful of pellets to her pot. *Wet them
with lighter fluid*, dad says, pointing to a bottle
and box. Sighing, he reminds me how to strike
a match, and I throw in the flame, lock her up.

As she catches—a twinkle in the darkness of her
rusted pupil—I think Hephaestus himself couldn't
have smithed a more beautiful mechanism. I look
at dad, and in the depths of his blue eyes, behind

his glasses, I see the shadow of Prometheus.

III.

Enter the younger sister, Enviro Mini: tall,
slender, and sleek. She perches in the kitchen,

the bolt-on hearth pad spread like a skirt before her.
Only 238 pounds, with a hopper capacity

of 48 pounds of pellets, she boasts a large ash pan
and a lovely personality. I unlock her door

with the wooden handle hanging by her side
(her eye is glass, too, but it's safe to look),

excavate the ash from her burn pot, and place
a single pellet inside her ignitor hole.

I close her up, hit power, and wait for her red button
(blinking) to stay constant as a lighthouse beam.

Her auger churns out a buttery glow,
and her smoke is sweet. My dad's voice echoes:

It's a good day when the stoves light…I tell ya,
I breathe easier in the morning when they start…

IV.

With thanks to Robert Hayden

Every morning, every winter, my dad woke
long before me—his footsteps silent to my
sleeping ears—to light the pellet stoves.
No one thanked him.

I'd walk to the kitchen, hover by the flame,
and ask for breakfast, never noticing
the soot that tinged his fingers. I'd nestle
in the basement, too; read a book in his

favorite chair, beside the burning machine,
its hum and friendly chatter filling the quiet.
My dad's love was humble, and our house
was sturdy. But what did I know—

what do I know—of what it takes to build
a home, let alone a fire?

V.

Dad's been outside, splitting wood for hours.

I'm curious, so I join him. I regard his sweat,
the stump, the maul—a grisly hybrid of axe
and sledgehammer. As he hands me the tool,
my grip on the long handle dips with the weight
of the head: metal, two-faced. One side heavy,
dull; the other sharp, chiseled. Almost like

the god. As I watch dad mime the swing, his
hands carve a portal in the air, allow me to peer
into a separate world—his world. One marked
by sore muscles, long days, and the male need
to provide. I am not part of that sphere. But I'm

here: knees bent, stance staggered, hips loose,
with both hands on the maul—one rests near
the head, the other towards the butt. Dad drops
a hunk of wood on the stump, and I raise. *Don't*
lift too far above your head, he says. *Let gravity*

take it—my hand slides down in a smooth arc,
enough force to cleave clean along the grain.
I want to do it again. Unsheathe this other side
of myself—

        that rips the maul from the stump as if
        I'd been doing it for years.

VI.

Every year, every winter, a storm comes.
The house is ill-equipped to face outages;
its power lines run through forest, near trees
laden with snow and ice. Generators are
expensive, so when the forecast heads south,

I help fill the tubs with water, check batteries
in the flashlights, locate the candles, open
the fridge as little as possible—and trudge out
to the wood pile. When the electricity goes,
the stoves die; smoke hangs from the ceilings

like the clouds outside, pregnant with heavy
darkness. We cough and shiver and wave
doors open, as cold air settles on the floors.
My father kneels in front of the fireplace—
on the sand-colored stones of our hearth—

beside him, a few logs lugged in with a pock-
marked leather sling—he throws three on the
grate, which gapes like a black-toothed maw,
shoves paper beneath. Reaching into the throat
of our home, he opens the flue—then lights—

—a match—

VII.

In darkness, a flame ignites. Hungry, feasts
on wood. In that alcove, the burning grows,
and we breathe, listening to our heartbeats.
I watch dad's face, flickering in shadow,
and wonder what it must be like to know
the ways of shovel, broom, poker, and tongs.
Maybe they only write that down in songs.

As I look at fire, I think of apples,
of chaos and exile—Eris and Eve—
primordial passion, women in shackles.
Hestia, on the hearth, gives dad a reprieve.
As his daughter, am I meant to believe
the story branded *London* on his shelf—
man versus nature—or do I read myself

and realize that women are elements
by virtue of being? Fire and earth,
water and air—these are the tenements
of our bodies. Yet the power of birth,
of babies, somehow detracts from our worth,
becomes our only purpose. And my hands
were never fit for needles; they demand

the forge, the hot honing of my own sword,
my body vestal and my mind virgin
to a spark we must tend and strive toward:
        anti-hero like Annie—oh Gwendolyn!
        Do women still wage war from the kitchen?
        How are battles greater based on color—
        when home we fight for is only—embers—

DOE *v.* DISTRICT: APPLE FOR THE DISTRICT

An erasure of the Roe v. Wade *U.S. Supreme Court decision syllabus (Jan. 22, 1973)*

A pregnant
criminal
mother
A childless
Doe pregnant
attacked
unprepared for parent- hood
A judge
held all
members of he r class
declar
e s war
o n those plain
Does
App l e pealed
app le cross- pealed
the D o e and
all *Held*
a peal o
f denial
app l
e deni e d
declarator

has standing the Does and all do not.

Contrary app le contention

repetition evading
exception rule
controversy

r age
refuse . err
no
defense against
h ate
The Does complain
more of which may occur

criminal except
criminality a life-saving the mother s
r age other
s violate

privacy
h ate cannot override
woman's
health and life, each of which
grows a s
woman approach
the end the
decision
the judgment

mother, may i choose

. life, may i
choose regulate proscribe
judgement
mother
i mean

i define

I decide
i recognize

E *v.* ADE

that criminal

affirmed in part and reversed

Nocturne-Elegy in New York City

I'm so tired I'm walking into walls. —J.B.

Wear your grief like a fur coat from Bergdorf
Goodman, amidst the dirt and homeless men.
Let it smother you like expensive mink,

and almost choke when you see her ghost
through those rotating, golden doors—let it
hit you like a taxi. The sight of the doorman

standing sentry; the lamps latticed in iron;
the store name engraved on smooth stone; let it
hold you hostage. Feel alone as some hollow

home beckons. Pretend to walk inside (and
maybe you do). Say her name beneath the
crystal chandeliers, and know this treasure

is too precious for your touch, spoils of the war
she fought: sewing needles strewn like swords
on the upholstery, each manicured room

a tomb for jewels, fine clothing, shoes
in every color and style—crypts stuffed with
decadent dead things. What rites are given

that allow entrance to this sacred space? I'm
a disturbance to the dust, the lacquered mahogany
and caramelized marble, yet somehow feel

as if part of this dazzling grandeur is mine.
Because of her. Pay your respects; I prefer
the filth outside. Let me paint this picture

in your mind: the ghost takes her leave
from that place, through those doors,
and maybe it's Christmas Eve. She goes home

late, exhausted, the retail industry at its
peak holiday season, after not hearing (or
pretending not to hear) customers whisper

bitch behind her back when she tells them
to depart the building. *That woman scares me
when she yells.* After getting paid less than

a man, she goes home and finds, as a woman,
her work is two-fold: cookies, plates of food,
and a host of gifts remain wrapped where

she left them (all prepared weeks in advance).
She puts on a feast and then it's off to midnight
mass and festivities with the godchildren 'til

two AM. She wakes at seven and prepares
breakfast: coffee, homemade stollen, fresh sliced
oranges for good luck. Peanut M&Ms and

chocolate kisses glisten in bowls as family
open stockings, then boxes upon boxes.
The ordeal takes hours, and brunch is eggs

benedict with mimosas. She lays out dinner at
four o'clock. Is this the fate of a matriarch?
Is this the parable my grandmother left me:

work yourself to death and die young
because you care. Because you're cursed with
capacity. Because you're caring for everyone

but yourself, numbing pain with pills and drink
'til your liver can't take it anymore. Deprive
the world of the sparkling stone you are—but let

this cycle end with me. Watch this matriarchy
of mothers past crumble at our feet. Spread
the ashes, and rise from them with me:

a new matriarch in the making.

***

A swan swims deep beneath the surface,
reaches her long neck to the muck,
pearl head nuzzling the silt,
the top soil—
the bedrock—
                    digging
                    digging
                    digging

Fourth 500 meters: Spring

Her strength spent, pale and faint, with pleading eyes
she gazed upon her father's waves and prayed,
"Help me my father, if thy flowing streams
have virtue! Cover me, O mother Earth!
Destroy the beauty that has injured me,
or change the body that destroys my life."

Before her prayer was ended, torpor seized
on all her body, and a thin bark closed
around her gentle bosom, and her hair
became as moving leaves; her arms were changed
to waving branches, and her active feet
as clinging roots were fastened to the ground—
her face was hidden with encircling leaves…

And thus the God;
"Although thou canst not be my bride, thou shalt
be called my chosen tree, and thy green leaves,
O Laurel! shall forever crown my brows,
be wreathed around my quiver and my lyre;
the Roman heroes shall be crowned with thee,
as long processions climb the Capitol
and chanting throngs proclaim their victories…"

—Ovid, "Daphne and Phoebus,"
Metamorphoses

On the Road to Ballyvaughan

Women go walking, over the stile, down the grass path to a hazel
grove, the twisted wood low on their heads, as if stepping into a fairy
land. Dappled canopy, moss and vines, soon give way to stone;
the trail forward, uncertain. Gray rocks, spread like mines, are sacred
to the people who call this place home. But us? We only see green
in forty shades—have yet to learn how time and memory

saturate the layered mountain-domes—all fish bones and memories,
petrified and pooled like cooled magma. It's best to hike with a hazel
rod, though we have none; limestone morphs into thicket, a green
labyrinth of hedge, nettle, and branch. The soft voices of fairies
trickle into our ears, we think, like water from a holy well: sacred,
healing, sought after for miles. Maze thins to meadow, with stones

never scarce. Seasons change here by how light touches stones,
not the turn of leaves. Cattle winter on hill tops. Genetic memory
weaves like flora through the grykes; gentians, orchids, sacred,
are blushing gums to fossil teeth. Our pockets clack with hazel-
nuts. Our shoes are covered in rock dust—star dust—is it fairy
dust? The scent of God's Tears, *Deora Dé*, intoxicates, a green,

constant incense. We see remnants of a village, swathed in green,
eaten by the earth but not completely swallowed, the stone
structures home to sweeping ferns, creeping ivy, as if the fairies
whisper: *an Drochshaol.* Tragedy engraved on collective memory.
Eerie as the facing shore, where the sea meets a girl named Hazel
and her father—the tide, rogue, rips him away. The town's sacred

steeple overflows with mourners. But the ocean, too, is sacred;
it hammers the cliffs with its fists, dark knuckles turning green—
no, aquamarine as they break. A canon's cacophony. We bite hazel-
nuts to make us wise. *Bean feasa.* But what are we to stone,
to the waves regurgitating the rusted carcass of a ship? Is the memory
of such things only guarded by that other crowd, fairies,

the wee folk who watch us now? In the middle of a field, a fairy
tree—whitethorn or blackthorn, regal as olive—stands alone, sacred,
its every root and limb protected; its trunk ringed with memories.
To pierce its bark, and watch it bleed—its blood not green,

but gold—would only lead to misfortune. From between stones,
stacked and snaking like tails of dragons, black eyes blink. Hazel

wands must be treacherous arms. Our memories are soaked in green.
Fairies light the way: candles in castle windows. Caves echo with
stone.
A butterfly lands on a sill, sacred, its wings the color of my
irises: hazel.

In Time of War & Plague

Population of Ballyvaughan, County Clare, Ireland (July 2022): 250 locals, 310 Ukrainian refugees

I.

The stones of the pier are gray. All the rocks here are gray.

She sits facing Galway Bay. In this moment she is a student
of art, absorbing inspiration from the distant mountains,
hiking the ones close by. A traveler, passing through.

She dangles her legs over the edge, nothing but air, water,
and sand below her feet. Gravity hungers. Her phone,
without her knowing, creeps from her pocket.

A tap on her shoulder. An accented voice alerts her
of the metal device making its escape. She looks down,
flustered, says thanks. Takes the phone in her hand,
looks up to see the stranger's back

retreating. A pink, striped shirt. Dancing long blond hair.

II.

In the local store, she buys herself a pair of red,
wool socks. She's tempted to buy a cone of soft serve, too.
They put a chocolate stick in it. As she debates this,
a little girl stands next to her, points at something, and speaks
in a language she doesn't recognize. The only word
she understands is *momma*—universal. Momma in question
is wrapped in a yellow rain jacket, carrying a basket
that contains a single item: a child-size pair of magenta rain boots.

This mother could be anyone. Like the ordinary fairy-folk
the townspeople talk about.

But as the mind asks questions—*who are you,*
why are you here—the answer is bare
on the woman's face.

Because we have nowhere else.

III.

At the height of summer, I flew across a sea,
chased the sunrise to new shores, new islands;
against all instinct, I left my family
to discover myself again in Ireland.

Four weeks, they said, to slow down, unwind.
The first week, I wrote and hiked each day;
the second week, I walked on Aran, blind
by rain—the third week I caught the plague.

I inhaled that ghost, felt him sit in my chest—
reach his arm up my throat—squeeze my breath—

> *I was bitten by a vampire—*
> *I was burning at the stake—*
> *I was lying in a coffin,*
> *sprouting wings from my shoulder blades—*

but the honeybees went about their way.

IV.

It had been a long time since she'd seen her grandmother, in dreams or otherwise. She paused to look at her, sitting in a chair in that red-walled living room, in her bathrobe and slippers and jammies. Her glasses perched on her nose. Her eyes—so sharp and with it—returned the stare. Her elbow balanced on an arm of the chair, and her hand rested on the side of her face—the exact shape she remembered…

In a rare moment in dreams, she took control of the narrative. She was fixated on her grandmother. "Are you real?" she asked.

Of course I'm real. Her grandmother did not speak aloud, though somehow, she knew this is what she said. And she believed her. She was so vivid in that instant. She took a few steps closer to her, conscious of the changes she'd gone through since she last saw her…

"Do you remember me?" she asked. She couldn't take her eyes off her grandmother. She sat on the floor in front of her, gazing up at her. A flush grew bright pink in her grandmother's cheek.

Of course I remember you. The sense of memories between them—potent bonds—still strong. *How could I forget.*

She took her eyes away from her grandmother, turned on the floor, and looked towards the TV. Still aware of her grandmother's presence behind her. Still wondering. The dream continued, back on script.

> She woke, covered in sweat, with words on her lips: *How could I forget.* Tried to savor that vision of her grandmother under her lids for as long as she could.
>
> The inlet, across the street from the house, had been filled with swans.

V.

If I die, bury me up there and then in a year's time when the newspapers have forgotten me, dig me up and plant me in Sligo.
—W.B. Yeats

Aches and fever dreams subside, and I surface.
Seven days pass. The same walls. I try to breathe
and ignore the ghost; to rest, not be nervous—
but I find another sickness ails me.
I walk the Flaggy Shore, and sense a sternness
at the sight of slender white on Lough Murree—
a lagoon I have somehow seen before.
Suddenly my dreams are knocking at the door.

I wonder if Yeats, pacing his tower, thought—
amid the thunder of war from his window—
that the stones around him were not enough.
I think I know that he dreamed of Sligo,
his country of the mind; island of the heart.
What luxury—what it means to have a home!
Every fiber of myself, tied to that place,
in a golden umbilical cord that fate

cannot cut. Three thousand miles of ocean—
but the same waves are beating on those beaches.
So thankful that my home is whole, not ruined—
that there's somewhere to return. In the reaches
of my heart, though, echoes the endless question:
to grab my pen by the hilt, and slash speeches—
or acknowledge that we, soldier or poet,
have little purchase on the tide of moment.

Katabasis

Take the yellow, bleached cutting board
that barely fits the width of fruit. Then
get the biggest knife and slice the middle
of the rosy leather. See that? A dribble
of juice so red it looks purple. Seeping
from the wound you made. You pause,

unsure how to avoid getting stains on
the cream countertop. As it keeps pooling,
press harder, 'til steel meets board. A squelch.
Dots of purple-red. Halves roll away
from each other, revealing the intricate inner:
glistening flesh, pulsing veins. You find
your hand—not the one holding the knife—
crawling to your chest, as if what lay
on the counter is not a fruit but what throbs

beneath your ribcage. As it beats, you watch
the life drain from bone-white cavities,
rubied catacombs.

> You think of maid Kore and her story.
> What if hell was a nice place to be?
> What if she loved Hades? If she saw that
>
> pomegranate and just had to hold it, *squeeze* it—
> when it started to bleed, can you blame her
> for wanting to raise it to her lips, to suck it
> dry as if it was a goblet of wine? To lick the
> chthonic rivulets racing down her fingers,
> her elbows, her chin—can she be blamed
>
> for sinking her teeth into fate? And is this fate
> or can she *take* the knife, the scythe,
> and carve herself anew from the remains.
> Not another girl being chased by a god—
> not a killer, not a queen—
>
> but whatever she wants to be.

Daphne and the Hydra

Head 1.

You know the myth: big snake lake monster
with nine heads, poisonous breath, and boiling
blood that would knock you dead from just
a whiff of its scent. As hard as you labor—
slice one neck and two more grow back—
you might just get the best of this beast.

And I'm only a tree. I can't comment on
the physical fight, but I feel a strange
comradery with this slimy foe. When I imagine
approaching her watery lair, I see from her
many eyes, heed her many voices, and think:
what a beautiful thing multiplicity must be.

Is she a demon, or is she me?

Head 2.

I'm not interested in killing, unless it's killing
the patriarchy. Specifically Apollo. He's the one
who turned me into a laurel tree. I used to be free,
a nymph running around doing what I pleased—

until that golden shadow descended, untouchable
as only a god, a man can be. No, I won't fight
this monster: like me, she has many branches,
many roots, never limited to just one identity—

all connected to the same trunk: ringed, knotted,
scarred, with some magic in her heart that I can't
help but admire: a willingness to go on: the fact that she
comes back, comes back, comes back.

Is she a demon, or is she me?

Head 3.

Imagine emerging from your lair,
another demigod shin-deep in your waters,
sword stuck in the muck—but this time

her. You could've sworn you saw
your faces flicker behind her eyes. She's something
in disguise. You tilt your heads as she

drowns her weapon. She doesn't flinch
from your gazes; instead stands, wrists
forward, palms up in a truce you can't deduce…
she's a new breed, and you concede

to fearing her, this monster-hero: like you, she knows
to weigh what she can give up, to what she might gain.

Is she a demon, or is she me?

Head 4.

Apollo only stole my leaves.
I transformed into the source:
the circlet itself that rests
on the heads of athletes.

I am laurel: I am woman: I am athlete:

my body is *capable* of birthing
but it's not *meant* for it: watch me
pull my own weight and the weight
of many: let these pages lift women
when they are let down: we are not
just the victors—we are the crown.

In that rowing shell, what do you see?

Is she a demon, or is she me?

Head 5.

Apollo only stole my ink—all poets owe *me*
for their bay leaves. I am woman: I am poet:
I am maker. My children are my verses,
just like Bradstreet: I am constantly pregnant

with thought—words kick my mind at night,
trick me to dream at day; their hearts beat fast
and demand to be born, splashing my screens
with piecemeal beginnings, or wait in the back
of my brain, 'til I deign to labor their lives
on the page. A pen is not just a weapon
in the hand of a woman: it's a pair of forceps
yanking life into the planet. This mother-writer:

is she a demon, or is she me?

Head 6.

And if I ever
become a mother—
by my own choice
or otherwise—
let this take root:
motherhood
is nothing to be despised.
Let *her* take root: a mother of
the future, fitting freedom, family,
her identities into no mold—
but the one
she shapes
for herself. *Is she a demon, or is she me?*

Head 7.

If I ever get beyond the tree phase,
loosen my bark and abandon the rigidity
I have adopted for so long based
on what's expected of me, I'd be
the type of lover that isn't picky
with her pickings: loving beauty
in whatever and whoever I see it.

I'd be Odysseus coming home
to Penelope, faithful at the loom;
a willing victim of the siren's croon;
Achilles raging for Patroclus—and who
never thought Helen was hot? This lover:

is she a demon, or is she me?

Head 8.

Glean what you want from this saga, reader.
I hand you this torch, carried from the ones

who came before us, to the ones yet to come.
It's up to you: take it. Reject it. Stare at it.

Might be worth it, might not. Some things
to alter, some things to keep. But if

there's an oath to keep, let it be this:
love yourself no matter what hounds you,

refuse to be a symbol, a myth, a monster or hero—
be what you *yearn* to be and change the narrative.

Life is a relay, and you're hunting divine prey:
is she a demon—

or is she you?

Head 9.

A blank slate for whatever comes next.

The Single Shell

An oar in each hand, one hull
keeping me afloat, I roll

to the catch, knees to my chest,
arms spread wide—try not to think

of the abyss below as blades glide
flat atop the surface. Not yet confident

to square, hover in air, then hook
that quicksilver. They say women

look more natural on the water.
Our bodies are always changing;

patience, control, rhythm, balance
are what we know best; an alchemical

process. To master the single shell—
both captain and crew—is to master

the soul. My careful strokes leave
puddles, dark and deep; pools whirl

in beats behind the rippling line
of my stern. Even aquatic creatures

can dream of flying. And me?
What might emerge when I shed

the various versions of myself—
something dying inside,

something wiser—monarch,
orange and black—

born.

Elysium

A woman, so darkened by the sun, that Apollo wishes she was his own.

Like all mortals, I come by river.
But in the boat, I man the oars,
and these waters are familiar.

When my mother dipped me
in the Styx, she held me up
by the wings. I've felt an ache

between my shoulders ever since.
So when I meet the god of death
at his gates, his onyx eyes flash

in remembrance. Above all, he
knows heroes need a home.
I pass the fields of Asphodel

untouched, hear the roar
of Tartarus, and open my eyes
to an island, so *blessed*.

Golden wheat rises to my hips.
My hands brush Queen Anne's
lace, purple thistle, and blue

chicory wildflowers. On rows
of vines, the grapes are hard
and sour. I walk a long, dirt path

towards a heaven made
just for me. The road, ending,
continues with train tracks.

Sarah C. Beckmann is from the Boston (MA) area and works at MIT in Cambridge, where she applies her writing skills in research communications. As a member of the Somerville Arts Council Board, she promotes arts initiatives in the Somerville community through a local grant program and the SomerWrites event series. In 2021 she published a poetry chapbook, *Naiad Blood*, and *The Race for Daphne* is her first full-length poetry collection.

Sarah continues crafting her poetry and draws inspiration from her experiences as an athlete and artist; her identity as a woman and an active member of her family and community; and her interests in genealogy and mythology. Nowadays you'll find her rowing out of Gentle Giant Rowing Club in Somerville, on the Mystic River.

She holds an MFA in Creative Writing from Emerson College, and was nominated for the Bill Knott Thesis Prize. Her work has been published previously by the City of Boston, the Academy of American Poets, Alternating Current Press, and *the Under Review.*

www.ingramcontent.com/pod-product-compliance
Lightning Source LLC
LaVergne TN
LVHW090536110826
845146LV00003B/1130

* 9 7 9 8 8 9 9 9 0 4 5 8 5 *